# TORY STEPHENS

# Loving Life Alcohol Free

*25 Instrumental Books to a Life You Love Alcohol Free*

# Contents

# 1

# Chapter 1

I ntroduction

Welcome to an instrumental list of phenomenal books to enjoy a life alcohol free. When I first started on my journey of living life free of alcohol I seemed to absorb every book on this topic, craving helpful tips, techniques and encouragement that I could get from others that had walked a similar path. I would have loved to have had a guide like this full of such insight and wisdom that all these books provide. This list is unique in that it provides a wide gamut of very different memoirs and approaches. One honors the 12-step program, another follows the Buddha path and others provide a more scientific approach of rewiring the brain in a very safe and subtle way. This last approach was the one that resonated profoundly and effectively with me. I love the fact that there are so many approaches and opportunities of recovery provided that are extremely accessible that can reach so many different ways a person prefers to reach their desired goal for a more fulfilled life. These books are so enlightening and if even one or some resonate they can truly change your life. Being sober and breaking free from the addictive cycle, to me, is as if you've been living in a dark cave with a dim candle to then step out into the bright sunshine with everything full of life and color. That's the best explanation I could provide of how I feel my life is then to now.

Here is a brief background of my life and why it has led me to have a desire to share these invaluable books with you! I grew up in Arkansas and to some that might seem like an undesirable place to live. To me, I look back and relish my time there. Folks are refreshingly down to earth. However, my upbringing was quite tumultuous as both of my parents suffered with addiction. I learned to walk delicately through life becoming a perfectionist and people pleaser. When I discovered alcohol at age 14, I was in love. Not only did it dissolve all of the problems that weighed heavy on my young and tender heart but I felt nice and snugly, pleasantly numb. I went on to graduate from the University of Arkansas with a Kinesiology degree. With this degree, most went to medical school but I chose to go into the Peace Corps in Zimbabwe. Living at my rural site for 2 years was extremely challenging and also completely fulfilling. However, when I would meet some of my fellow Peace Corps Volunteers in Harare, the city of Zimbabwe, we would all get wasted. Every.Single.Time. I was starting to see a pattern at this point in my life that my drinking was more than likely going to be a problem. After I finished Peace Corps I moved to San Francisco to pursue a career in the fitness industry. I became a personal trainer and created my own business. I also became a registered yoga instructor and you would think with all of this new enlightenment that alcohol would have organically faded away. Unfortunately, this was not the case. In fact, it was farther from the truth. I had learned to deal with all of my problems that came my way by the numbing effects of alcohol and gaining only the numbing and eventually debilitating effect of it. Unfortunately, I was numbing everything. It became VERY apparent it wasn't working the way it used to as my body craved more and more and

I began to go down a rabbit hole. My marriage and family relationships were suffering immensely and this is where I would hit rock bottom because my relationships are the most important thing to me in my life. So, my search began to cultivate a sober free life and I was determined to love it. That was my ultimate goal. Doing it was another story. I must say that I set the stage with all of my yoga training, meditation, etc. so that when the right formula came along (which are in many of these books below) it resonated and I'm so happy to say I have been sober free for five and a half years as I write this book. I hope that some or all of these books can resonate with you or a loved one. It would bring me great joy if these books helped just one beautiful soul. I mean that from the bottom of my heart. I hope and trust you'll enjoy them as much as I did.

# 2

# Chapter 2

K ick the Drink...Easily
    by Jason Vale

This book will really make you think. His approach is very refreshing. He has an interesting insight stating that there is no such thing as an alcoholic and there is no such disease as alcoholism! Some might feel strongly about this statement but one thing is for sure, you'll definitely see alcoholism in a completely different way after reading this book. Very enlightening to say the least. This book is a big-time eye-opener as it will challenge you to see alcohol in a completely different way as well as how society accepts it. It will challenge the way you view alcohol as our society has been conditioned to accept alcohol as a normal substance even though it's such a major cause of many of today's social problems and a wide range of health issues. It also helps you discover that cutting it out of your life will allow you to enjoy it so much more, in fact, more than you could ever imagine.

3

# Chapter 3

The Easy Way to Control Alcohol
by Alan Carr

This is one of the books that really hit the nail on the head for me. I was very skeptical at first but as I read on, his perspective began to resonate and new insight gained was undeniable. Is this a miracle book, I asked myself? Perhaps, but I did go into it with a very hopeful and open mind. He has many other books with one specifically for women. Same technique but addresses particular difficulties women can face when it comes to drinking. The technique explains why you might feel the need to drink and explains a straightforward step by step guide to release you from the grip of alcohol. What really resonated with me in this book is I didn't feel shamed into needing to be alcohol-free and most importantly no scare tactics and I felt as if it was coming from a straightforward and unconditional loved one. This truly was my turning point after reading this book. Pretty incredible stuff.

4

# Chapter 4

**A**lcohol lied to me: the intelligent way to escape alcohol addiction
**by Craig Beck**

This is another empowering book where the author discovers that you don't have to label yourself and go to exhausting meetings to become free of alcohol and sustain it. I enjoyed how this book explains how he slowly discovered the truth about alcohol and addiction and all the lies he previously believed. This method is unique in that you don't have to declare yourself an alcoholic. It's a permanent solution and cure. I also love that no willpower is required. In this book he treats the source of the problem not just the symptoms. I appreciated how this read is presented in a non-judgmental and caring way.

# 5

# Chapter 5

**R**ecovery 2.0 Move Beyond Addiction and Upgrade Your Life
**By Tommy Rosen**

I like the fact that in this book the author covers the whole gamut of how many people are suffering from some form of addiction. Whether it be social media, food, drink, drugs and even exercise! The list goes on…With over 20 years of recovery and working professionally with others, this author has uncovered core elements to recovery and healing which is what he refers to as recovery 2.0. In the book he shares his past struggles with addiction along with powerful revelations. With This profound knowledge and experience, he implements tried and true tools to break free from the shackles that stand in the way of feeling like our true and authentic self. The self that we came here to be. Rossen does work off of the 12-step program yet I feel he is much more open minded and holistic in this approach. So, if the 12-step program resonates with you, I would definitely suggest this book.

6

# Chapter 6

Why You Drink and How to Stop
By Veronica Valli

I feel like this is a highly researched book and is perfect for people with addiction that need to know the why and how. This book really clarifies some of the misconceptions and false information that surrounds addiction. This book brings it all together with relevant information to help someone struggling and looking for a life raft. It also provides guidance for family and friends. With all of Valli's diligent research, it can provide great peace of mind and clarity for those in addiction and people that support them.

7

# Chapter 7

This Naked Mind: Control Alcohol, Find Freedom, Discover Happiness and Change Your Life
By Annie Grace

Grace discusses the concept of how most can't imagine their life without their crutch that alcohol has become. They resist change because they fear losing the "fun" alcohol will bring and of course the stress relief associated with alcohol even though it can lead to more stress, anxiety and trouble. Assuming giving it up will include being deprived and miserable. Yet, this book offers a fresh new perspective as she discusses the psychological and neurological components of alcohol use based on latest science research and also demonstrates the relevance of social, cultural and industry factors that support the dependence of alcohol in all of us. Chopped full of interesting eye-openers on the reasons why we drink, this book will provide great insight to the shocking role of alcohol in our culture and how the stigma of alcoholism and recovery is the very thing that keeps people from getting the help they need. She also shares her transparent and personal story which always provides great solace for us seeking normalcy even through the healing and recovery process.

8

# Chapter 8

R ewired: A Bold New Approach to Addiction and Recovery
By Erica Spiegelman

This author is an addiction expert and focuses on self-actualization that will guide you toward being physically sober but also mentally, emotionally and spiritually sober by learning to become familiar with and identify key characteristics within yourself which include authenticity, gratitude, being honest with yourself and understanding and need for solitude at times. This book helps us build a healthy and safe space to support our own recovery and we can then rewrite negative behaviors that result in addiction. I also like to mention that the author says you could use this in conjunction with the 12-step program or in place of the 12-step program. Most importantly, Spiegelman offers a more holistic approach that helps to create a very personal action plan that is right only for you.

# 9

## Chapter 9

S ober Curious
**By Ruby Warrington**

In this book I felt as if I was reading my own life story. It's what most of us find hard to ignore these days whether we have a "problem" with alcohol or not. I mean, we do yoga, we workout, we drink green juice, we meditate, we take care of ourselves etc etc. Yet at the end of a long day we "treat" ourselves to a drink. Or if we're in an awkward social situation, we drink. Or we have a bad day… you get the picture. One glass of wine turns into two turns into a bottle. But what it really gets down to is how alcohol really makes us feel. For me, I felt like I was a gerbil on a wheel. The author describes this exactly. Warrington goes on to invite us to question what our lives would be like if we did stop drinking on autopilot? Or stopped completely. Really different, much much better it turns out. And again, I speak from experience. This book is a steady and bold guide to help you choose to live hangover free. This book draws on good research, great interviews in a personal narrative that are extremely relatable. It also breaks down the myths that keep us drinking. This book is empowering and can transform people's relationship with alcohol so we can lead our life with the utmost freedom.

10

# Chapter 10

A Happier Hour, Up All Day and Chameleon
By Rebecca Weller

I have a special place in my heart for Bex Weller which is why I've suggested all three of her books. This memoir is so raw and all too relatable allowing me to feel like I wasn't the only one that had suffered from addiction and craved so desperately to live life fully without it. She also has an online community called "Sexy Sobriety" that I joined and found extremely invaluable when I decided to get sober for good. She provides support, drink recipes and inspiring interviews with folks in the same boat. This is what started my sobriety journey and with her 90 day course I felt incredibly supported and encouraged that I could do it.

Up All Day is a sequel to her first book and examines her deep desire to be a writer. With no hangovers holding her back and nowhere to hide can she find the courage to confront her secret lifelong dream? She discovers that her hard won sobriety will only take her so far and

14

what comes next is up to her. It's an uplifting story for anyone who has ever had to conquer themselves in order to conquer their dreams. Because our biggest challenge in life and creating our fullest potential is one that takes place with deep self-knowing and reflection.

Chameleon: Confessions of a Former People Pleaser resonated so much with me as I too have overcome being held captive (by only myself) of being a people-pleaser. She explains so eloquently and clearly how the need to please is one of the sneakiest drinking triggers leading to the disease to please. She goes on to say that she is a former people pleaser but before that her pesky little need to be liked meant she was terrified of being a burden, or doing anything that might hurt somebody's feelings, and at the slightest confrontation would freeze or run. In this book she encourages one to take their power back. She explores the many clumsy, humiliating and ultimately liberating lessons we might experience along the way, and how each of us can begin to build self worth and certain confidence. She also emphasizes the danger of giving our power away to others and the beauty of finding our way back to ourselves. Truly magical.

# 11

# Chapter 11

**T**he Unexpected Joy of Being Sober
**By Catherine Gray**

First off, I absolutely love this book title. I couldn't find it more fitting for my journey as well. I knew, like Gray, that life would be better on the other side. It was just grappling with the how? I appreciate that her writing is so personal. It takes you to a comfort level that one can resonate with. It is refreshingly honest and transparent. What she says you are certain is our truth. This book is great for anyone pondering whether you would like to quit or not. Allowing yourself to check in and truly see if what you're doing is allowing you to live your best self in our life.

12

# Chapter 12

D rinking: A Love Story
  **Caroline Knapp**

This book really hit home as Carolyn began drinking at a young age like myself. She learned that creating "liquid armor" was a way to protect from all of life's difficulties. She was also able to function at a high level even though she was struggling deeply with addiction. This can sometimes provide an illusion for those in this high functioning situation. It's an extremely candid memoir. Knapp offers important insights all across the gamut. About life itself and how we learn to cope with it.

13

# Chapter 13

**D**ry: A Memoir
     **By Augusten Burroughs**

Burroughs is one of my favorite authors for many reasons. Mainly for his wicked humor and extraordinary writing. I delved right into this memoir that takes you on a rollercoaster of emotions. From happy to sad, laughing to crying and of course despair to hope. It's a heartbreaking story of his life circumnavigating his deep and intense struggles with alcohol. In the end, you're surprised he survives. Very entertaining and compelling with his detailed encounters. This Memoir is moving as it is funny, as heartbreaking as it is true. It is a story of love, loss and finally, finding his truth.

14

# Chapter 14

**D**runk Mom
**By Jowita Bydlowska**

Many have lived this before. Quit drinking, felt great, then… the special occasion to just have one celebratory drink. Then, on the proverbial gerbil wheel again.  In this at times tough to read story, Bydlowska gives great detail of the ways substance abuse took control of her life. The binges and blackouts, shame and taking enormous risks- as well as her fight to find a sober free life as a young mother. This brave memoir shines a light on the convoluted logic of an addicted mind and the incredible and powerful transformation from love of one's child. Provides great hope for those struggling in similar ways.

# 15

## Chapter 15

B lackout: **Remembering the Things I Drank to Forget**
**By Sarah Hepola**

This memoir is so transparent with great humor intertwined. A story of a woman who accidentally found herself in a new kind of adventure, the sober life she never wanted.

Hepola felt alcohol was the end all be all to life itself. She felt it was essentially the right to the 21st century woman. However, there was a price tag attached. Often blacking out, literally waking up having no idea what had happened the night before. Apologizing in numerous vague ways because she couldn't remember what to apologize for.

This honest and poignant memoir will resonate with anyone who has been forced to create a new stage, a new life in the face of necessary change.

20

16

# Chapter 16

Lit: A Memoir
By Mary Karr

Mary Karr is a pioneer in the memoir world. Her first book, The Liar's Club, kick started the memoir revolution. Lit: A Memoir explores the raw and real side of having a life completely controlled by alcohol. The struggles to recover, and eventually finding the spiritual side breaking free of the vicious cycle. Karr's story is very intense, some might say horrid, but eventually with the guidance of many dear souls she trusts, she finds her way in life sober and living the life she felt God meant for her to always have.

17

# Chapter 17

**G**irl Walks Out of Bar
**By Lisa Smith**

Lisa Smith was a successful lawyer until addiction took over her life. What was once a way she escaped her insecurities as a teenager bled into her life as an attorney due to her extremely high workload and insurmountable stress. Her memoir provides a clear story of her spiraling out of control to then find her way to her path of healing and recovery over addiction.

18

# Chapter 18

**B** etween Breaths: A Memoir of Panic and Addiction
**By Elizabeth Vargas**

Some might remember Elizabeth Vargas as a former ABC 20/20 anchor. She bravely shares her alcohol addiction and anxiety disorder in an incredibly honest and emotional memoir. She tells how growing up with anxiety and how she learned to cope the best way possible eventually turning to alcohol for a release from this uncomfortable and painful reality. She admits how she lived in denial about her reality with addiction, and how kept her dependency a secret for so long. She recounts her time in rehab and sustaining her sobriety while trying to maintain balance with her career and parenting. Vargas conveys great honesty and hope in her deeply raw book.

19

# Chapter 19

**M** **rs D is Going Without**
**By Lotta Dann**

This book would be very encouraging to anyone who feels overwhelmed by secrets that control their life. Mrs. D is dependent on alcohol but a very nice, respectable and articulate person but is consumed by addiction. Sound familiar? In this transparent and relatable memoir, Dann shares the journey from horrible, shameful existence to a self-respecting sober person. This memoir is an inspirational story of self-transformation and covers the entirety of an unexpected turn of events Mrs D took in the first year of her sobriety to discover the incredible and unexpected online support that came through her confessional blog, a blog intended to be a private online journal but turned into something extraordinary.

# 20

# Chapter 20

D rink: The Intimate Relationship Between Women and Alcohol
**By Ann Dowsett Johnston**

In this well-researched and insightful book Johnston chronicles her own destructive patterns with alcohol, her recovery and explores unsettling and disturbing trends the way society views women's relationship to alcohol. A really important book for anyone interested in women's health and addiction issues. Some of the stories are heartbreaking yet important to read especially to better understand the debilitating aspects of addiction. A game-changing perspective at one of our culture's hidden problems. This book is honest, courageous and very inspiring.

21

# Chapter 21

In the Realm of Hungry Ghosts: Close Encounters with Addiction
By Gabor Mate

This book is not only timely relevant but a profound eye-opening look at the epidemic of addictions in our society, telling us why we are so prone to them and why what is needed to liberate ourselves from their vise grip on our emotions and behaviors.

Gabor Mate is a physician and many of his patients are at the far end of the spectrum, many struggling with all kinds of addictions. Drugs, alcohol, tobacco work, food, sex, gambling and excessive an inappropriate spending is often his question to what is so off with our lives that we seek such self-destructive ways to comfort ourselves? He asks why it is so difficult to stop these habits even as they wreak havoc on our relationships, health and trash our lives. By observing an intensely close look on drug addiction with his patients he also examines his own life and history of compulsive behavior. He intertwines the stories of real people who have struggled with addiction with the most current research on addiction and how it works in the brain. Providing cutting-edge scientific findings, Dr Mate sheds light on addiction as one of life's perplexing human frailties. He creates a compassionate approach to helping people addicted to addressing the main reason why they choose addiction to fill a deep void.

22

# Chapter 22

Eight Step Recovery: Using the Buddha's Teachings to Overcome Addiction
By Valerie Mason

Humans have always had a tendency toward addiction. All of us can struggle with this tendency, but for many it can lead to the destruction of their lies, through obsessive and compulsive behavior. It's no surprise that addiction is everywhere we look. We live in a world where many of us self-medicate and respond to the stresses of life turning to anything that can alleviate that suffering in an attempt to crawl out and provide some happiness. Fortunately recovery is widespread too. In this approach, Buddhist teachings offer understanding that's how the mind works and tools for helping the mind that is vulnerable to addiction and ways to overcome addiction and obsessive behavior, cultivating a calm and clear mind without anger and resentment. For some the Buddhist teachings offer a passive recovery. This way can provide a more fulfilling life. The 8 steps in this book take you away from the trouble caused by addictive behavior that can help you unravel these drives to discover a more fulfilling and satisfying way of living.

29

23

# Chapter 23

**S**ober Stick Figure: A Memoir
    **By Amber Tozer**

This book is refreshing and unique as Tozer tells her story with stick figure art. Her story is told with self-deprecating wit and often cringe-worthy stories with a feeling of kindness towards others and finally in sobriety and kindness to herself. It's a very uplifting book that provides hope to her incredibly successful career in comedy.

24

# Chapter 24

A Place Called Self
### By Stephanie Brown

Dr. Brown is an addiction researcher and therapist that offers women a map to find their way through the twists and turns in sobriety. For many women being new to sobriety or even well into their sobriety with all of its accomplishments and new found happiness can also be a lonely and unsatisfying experience. Often feeling isolated and lonely can potentially set in. Here the pioneering therapist Doctor Brown helps readers understand that leaving behind the numbing comfort of alcohol and other drugs and addictions you have to face yourself sometimes for the first time. This book contains personal stories which allow the reader to not feel so alone as well as guide gently. Dr. Brown helps a person unravel the painful and confusing truth as well as the roller coaster of feelings and the process of creating a new true sense of self. One that has always been there since birth but has been blanketed by addiction.

25

# Chapter 25

T he Sober Revolution
**By Sarah Turner and Lucy Rocca**

This book encourages one to take a hard look at oneself to see if their life is truly what they are loving. When it comes to alcohol a lot of people find it challenging to practice moderation and become stuck in a vicious cycle of blame, shame and guilt. In this empowering book Turner and Rocca help you examine your relationship with alcohol and provide insight and advice into overcoming this addiction. It also explores the myths behind this socially acceptable yet often destructive habit and through personal experiences of alcohol abuse and its harsh impacts on relationships, careers and finances. It invites one to examine their relationship with alcohol and its impacts on their life.

26

# Chapter 26

**A**lcohol and You: How to Control and Stop Drinking
By Lewis David

I found this to be an empowering and enlightening book as it provides everything you need to self diagnose alcohol problems as well as find the solution that works best for you. David is a leading addictions therapy practitioner and also a best-seller author of the 10-day alcohol detox plan and as well as the mindfulness of 4 alcohol recovery. His research with over 100 clients in treatment revealed the ideal ways to overcome problematic drinking. In this groundbreaking book, he passes on that knowledge to you. It's also written in a very uplifting and easy-to-follow format that will leave you feeling inspired, fully informed and looking forward to your future. Some of the things it clearly explains that I found fascinating are: The best scientifically proven ways to reduce or quit drinking. How to self-diagnose alcohol dependence in minutes. How to motivate yourself to change and enjoy the process. How to decide whether cutting down or quitting is right for you. Medications and strategies to help deal with Cravings. The best free support to help maintain your progress over time.

## Conclusion

Many of these books truly did change my life. I really appreciated the memoirs as it allowed me to feel like I was in good company. All the authors I found incredibly transparent, courageous and brave sharing their deepest darkest part of their life with the world. I appreciated this so much and revealed how each one, on their very different paths, made it to the other side. The common theme I found was that life challenges will always come our way, as it should, but that life, clear and sober, is just better. I can't emphasize enough how I never thought I could do it. But I can honestly say with great conviction that I truly don't think about drinking anymore. My life is too complete. I still get the roller coaster of emotions but find that with each obstacle, life is offering the choice to evolve and create more of what I truly want and desire into my life. My hope is that if one so desires to find their path to living alcohol free they will find great epiphanies, insight or even solace in these incredible books. Be well and remember, I was as surprised as anyone to discover that life can be so authentically joyous living alcohol-free.

If you found this book helpful, I'd be very appreciative if you left a favorable review for the book on Amazon!

## Resources

Beck, C. (2017, January 9). *Alcohol lied to me: The intelligent way to escape alcohol addiction*. Amazon. Retrieved July 27, 2022, from https://www.amazon.com/

Brown, S. (2004, July 20). *A Place Called Self*. Amazon. Retrieved July 27, 2022, from https://www.amazon.com/

Burroughs, A. (2013, April 23). *Dry. A Memoir*. Amazon. Retrieved July 27, 2022, from https://www.amazon.com/

Bydlowska, J. (2014, May 27). *Drunk Mom*. Amazon. Retrieved July 27, 2022, from https://www.amazon.com/

Carr, A. (2013, September 1). *The Easy Way to Control Alcohol*. Google. Retrieved July 27, 2022, from https://www.allencarr.com

Dann, L. (2014, October 1). *Mrs D is Going Without*. Amazon. Retrieved July 27, 2022, from https://www.amazon.com/

David, L. (2017, April 13). *Alcohol and You: How to Control and Stop Drinking*. Amazon. Retrieved July 27, 2022, from https://www.amazon.com/

Grace, A. (2018, January 2). *This Naked Mind: Control Alcohol, Find Freedom, Discover Happiness and Change Your Life*. Amazon. Retrieved July 27, 2022, from https://www.amazon.com/

Gray, C. (2018, December 18). *The Unexpected Joy of Being Sober*. Amazon. Retrieved July 27, 2022, from https://www.amazon.com/

Hepola, S. (2016, June 7). *Blackout: Remembering the Things I Drank to Forget*. Amazon. Retrieved July 27, 2022, from https://www.amazon.c

om

Johnston, A. (2014, June 24). *Drink: The Intimate Relationship Between Women and Alcohol*. Amazon. Retrieved July 27, 2022, from https://www.amazon.com/

Karr, M. (2010, June 29). *Lit: A Memoir*. Amazon. Retrieved July 27, 2022, from https://www.amazon.com/

Knapp, C. (1996, May 2). *Drinking: A Love Story*. Amazon. Retrieved July 27, 2022, from https://www.amazon.com/

Mason-John, V. (2018, September 18). *Eight Step Recovery: Using the Buddha's Teachings to Overcome Addiction*. Amazon. Retrieved July 27, 2022, from https://www.amazon.com/

Mate, G. (2009, January 6). *In the Realm of Hungry Ghosts: Close Encounters with Addiction*. Amazon. Retrieved July 27, 2022, from https://www.amazon.com/

Rocca & Turner, L. S. (2015, September 27). *The Sober Revolution*. Amazon. Retrieved July 27, 2022, from https://www.amazon.com/

Rossen, T. (2014, October 21). *Recovery 2.0 Move Beyond Addiction and Upgrade Your Life*. Amazon. Retrieved July 27, 2022, from https://www.amazon.com/

Smith, L. (2016, June 7). *Girl Walks Out of Bar*. Amazon. Retrieved July 27, 2022, from https://www.amazon.com/

Spiegelman, E. (2015, April 28). *Rewired: A Bold New Approach to*

*Addiction and Recovery.* Amazon. Retrieved July 27, 2022, from https://www.amazon.com/

Tozer, A. (2016, June 2). *Sober Stick Figure: A Memoir.* Amazon. Retrieved July 27, 2022, from https://www.amazon.com/

Vale, J. (2011, March 20). *Kick the Drink. . .Easily!* Amazon. Retrieved July 27, 2022, from https://www.amazon.com/

Valli, V. (2013, August 10). *Why You Drink and How to Stop.* Amazon. Retrieved July 27, 2022, from https://www.amazon.com/

Vargas, E. (2017, September 12). *Between Breathes: A Memoir of Panic and Addiction.* Amazon. Retrieved July 27, 2022, from https://www.amazon.com/

Warrington, R. (2018, December 31). *Sober Curious.* Amazon. Retrieved July 27, 2022, from https://www.amazon.com/

Weller, R. (2016, September 2). *A Happier Hour.* Amazon. Retrieved July 27, 2022, from https://www.amazon.com

Weller, R. (2019, September 6). *Up All Day.* Amazon. Retrieved July 27, 2022, from https://www.amazon.com/

Weller, R. (2021, August 1). *Chameleon.* Amazon. Retrieved July 27, 2022, from https://www.amazon.com/